HAL•LEONARD
INSTRUMENTAL
PLAY-ALONG

C000246566

HIGH SCHOOL MUSICAL

How To Use The CD Accompaniment:
A melody cue appears on the right channel only. If your CD player has a balance adjustment, you can adjust the volume of the melody by turning down the right channel.

ISBN 1-4234-1283-4

Disney characters and artwork © Disney Enterprises, Inc.

Walt Disney Music Company

DISTRIBUTED BY

HAL•LEONARD®
CORPORATION

7777 W. BLUEMOUND RD. P.O. BOX 13819 MILWAUKEE, WI 53213

For all works contained herein:
Unauthorized copying, arranging, adapting, recording or public performance is an infringement of copyright.
The purchase or rental of these materials does not constitute a license to perform this play.
Performance without a license is a violation of United States copyright law and an actionable federal offence.

Visit Hal Leonard Online at
www.halleonard.com

Song	Page	CD Track
Bop to the Top	4	1
Breaking Free	6	2
Get'cha Head in the Game	8	3
I Can't Take My Eyes Off of You	10	4
Start of Something New	12	5
Stick to the Status Quo	14	6
We're All in This Together	16	7
What I've Been Looking For	18	8
When There Was Me and You	20	9
B♭ Tuning Notes		10

◆ BOP TO THE TOP

FLUTE

Words and Music by RANDY PETERSEN
and KEVIN QUINN

© 2005 Wonderland Music Company, Inc.
All Rights Reserved   Used by Permission

❷ BREAKING FREE

FLUTE

Words and Music by
JAMIE HOUSTON

© 2005 Walt Disney Music Company
All Rights Reserved   Used by Permission

7

❸ GET'CHA HEAD IN THE GAME

Flute

Words and Music by RAY CHAM,
GREG CHAM and ANDREW SEELEY

© 2005 Walt Disney Music Company and Five Hundred South Songs
All Rights Reserved   Used by Permission

(Spoken:) Get - 'cha, get - 'cha, get - 'cha, get - 'cha head in the game. __ Whoo! ___

◆ 4 I CAN'T TAKE MY EYES OFF OF YOU

FLUTE

Words and Music by MATTHEW GERRARD
and ROBBIE NEVIL

© 2005 Walt Disney Music Company
All Rights Reserved   Used by Permission

◆ START OF SOMETHING NEW

FLUTE

Words and Music by MATTHEW GERRARD
and ROBBIE NEVIL

© 2005 Walt Disney Music Company
All Rights Reserved   Used by Permission

◆ STICK TO THE STATUS QUO

FLUTE

Words and Music by DAVID N. LAWRENCE
and FAYE GREENBERG

© 2005 Walt Disney Music Company
All Rights Reserved   Used by Permission

◆ 7 WE'RE ALL IN THIS TOGETHER

FLUTE

Words and Music by MATTHEW GERRARD
and ROBBIE NEVIL

© 2005 Walt Disney Music Company
All Rights Reserved   Used by Permission

◆ 8 WHAT I'VE BEEN LOOKING FOR

FLUTE

Words and Music by ANDY DODD
and ADAM WATTS

© 2005 Walt Disney Music Company
All Rights Reserved   Used by Permission

❾ WHEN THERE WAS ME AND YOU

FLUTE

Words and Music by
JAMIE HOUSTON

Slowly

© 2005 Walt Disney Music Company
All Rights Reserved   Used by Permission